AI Made Si

Empowering the Next G

Discover, Learn, Create: Unlocking AI's Potential for Curious Minds of All Ages

Nitin Panwar

Table of Contents

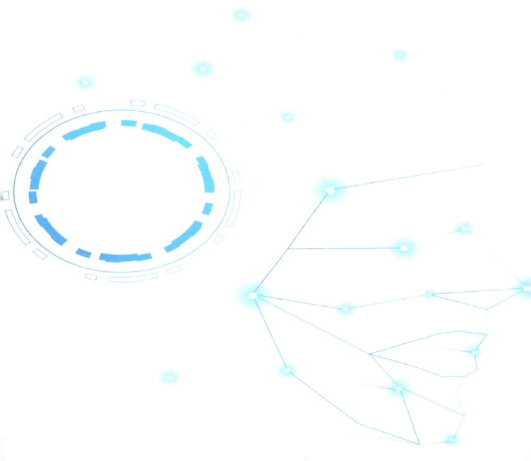

The Mind Behind the Words

Nitin Panwar is an AI enthusiast, thought leader, and author passionate about exploring the limitless possibilities of artificial intelligence while ensuring it remains a force for good.

With a proven track record of leading digital transformation and innovation at global organizations, Nitin brings a unique blend of expertise in AI and a commitment to empowering individuals and organizations to thrive in the age of technology.

Nitin's first book, **Humintel: The Synergy of Human and Artificial Intelligence**, laid the foundation for his mission to explore how AI and human intelligence can work in harmony to amplify creativity, solve global challenges, and build a better future.

In this, his second book, Nitin continues this mission, focusing on empowering the next generation to understand, embrace, and use AI to shape the future in positive and ethical ways.

His work emphasizes the importance of using AI ethically, responsibly, and creatively to amplify human ingenuity and solve real-world challenges.

Nitin's vision is clear: to inspire people from all walks of life to embrace AI as a tool for empowerment and growth. Through his writing, Nitin aims to make AI accessible to everyone, especially young minds, breaking down complex concepts into simple, actionable insights. His goal is to inspire the next generation to see AI not as a threat but as a partner in tackling global challenges and enhancing human potential.

He wants to equip them with the knowledge and skills to leverage AI to create solutions, unlock new possibilities, and build a future where technology and humanity coexist in harmony.

Nitin's work is rooted in the belief that the future is bright for those who embrace AI with curiosity, responsibility, and purpose.

He encourages individuals to use AI ethically, to innovate creatively, and to approach challenges with a sense of empathy and accountability.

Empowering the Next Generation

When he's not writing or driving transformation projects, Nitin is passionate about teaching, mentoring, and exploring innovative ways to bridge technology and human potential.

Through his work, he continues to encourage individuals to think boldly, act with purpose, & build a future where technology humanity thrive together.

AI is the canvas; the next generation are the artists, painting a future where imagination knows no limits.

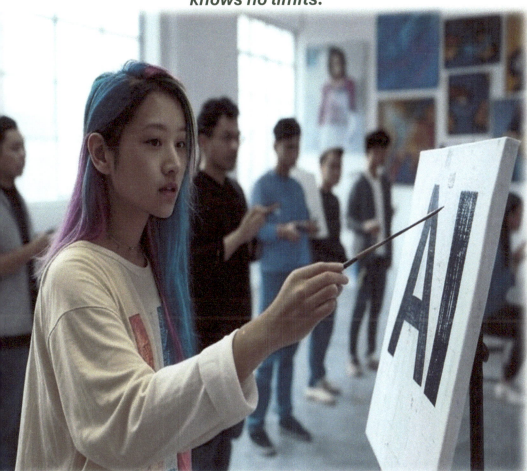

Introduction: A Vision for Empowering the Next Generation

The world as we know it is evolving at an unprecedented pace, and at the heart of this transformation lies artificial intelligence (AI). Once confined to the realm of science fiction, AI now touches nearly every aspect of our lives, from the way we communicate to how we diagnose diseases, grow our food, and envision a more sustainable planet. But with great power comes great responsibility and an incredible opportunity to reshape our world for the better.

This book is born out of the belief that the true potential of AI is not just in its ability to automate tasks or generate insights but in its capacity to address some of humanity's most pressing challenges. Climate change, access to quality healthcare, equitable education, and ethical dilemmas are just a few of the global issues where AI can play a transformative role. Yet, for this potential to be realized, we must empower the next generation, students, educators, and young innovators to not only understand AI but also to shape its future responsibly.

Demystifying AI for All: Despite its growing presence in our daily lives, AI often remains a complex and intimidating subject for many. Terms like "machine learning," "neural networks," and "data algorithms" can feel like a foreign language, particularly to young minds. This book aims to bridge that gap by breaking down the fundamentals of AI into accessible, relatable concepts. By doing so, it seeks to inspire curiosity and foster a deeper understanding of how AI works, how it is applied, and how it can be leveraged to create positive change.

Through real-world examples and practical applications, readers will explore how AI is being used to improve healthcare outcomes, enhance learning experiences, combat environmental crises, and address ethical dilemmas. The stories and case studies included are not just about technology—they are about people, ideas, and the limitless possibilities that emerge when we combine human ingenuity with the power of AI.

A Call to Action for the Next Generation: This is more than just a book about technology; it is a call to action. The students of today are the architects of tomorrow, and their voices, creativity, and ethics will shape the AI-driven world we are building. By equipping young readers with the knowledge and tools to engage with AI, we can ensure that this technology evolves in ways that reflect the values of equity, inclusivity, and sustainability.

The chapters ahead are designed to spark inspiration and provide guidance. You will journey through the ways AI is addressing climate change, revolutionizing education, advancing healthcare, and challenging us to rethink what it means to be human. Each chapter will not only highlight the possibilities but also encourage critical thinking about the ethical implications and responsibilities that come with harnessing AI's power.

Why This Matters Now: The urgency of today's challenges demands bold, innovative solutions, and AI offers an unparalleled toolkit for addressing them. But the success of these efforts depends on our ability to prepare the next generation to be thoughtful leaders and collaborators in this transformation. As the stewards of AI's future, young people have the unique opportunity to ensure that technology serves humanity's highest aspirations rather than its narrowest interests.

Together, we can envision a world where AI doesn't just solve problems but fosters connections, amplifies human creativity, and empowers communities. This book is an invitation to imagine that future and to take the first steps toward building it.

Your Journey Begins Here

Whether you are a student, teacher, parent, or simply someone curious about the possibilities of AI, this book is for you. It is for anyone who believes in the potential of technology to make the world a better place and who wants to be part of that journey. Let us embark on this exploration together, with open minds, bold ideas, and a shared commitment to empowering the next generation to lead us into a brighter, more equitable future.

Part 1: The Foundation

Artificial Intelligence (AI). Just saying the words might make you think of sci-fi movies, sleek robots, or complex algorithms you'll never understand. But let's pause for a second. AI isn't some distant, futuristic concept anymore; it's right here, shaping how we live, work, and even think. And whether you're already fascinated by it or just curious about what the fuss is all about, there's no escaping its growing influence.

Here's the thing: understanding AI doesn't have to feel overwhelming. You don't need a computer science degree to grasp what's going on. At its heart, AI is about teaching machines to do things that typically require human intelligence. Think of it as creating tools that can learn, adapt, and make decisions; sometimes faster and better than we can. It's behind things like the recommendations you get on Netflix, voice assistants like Siri or Alexa, and even systems that help doctors diagnose diseases.

But this isn't just about technology, it's about people, too. AI doesn't exist in a vacuum. It's intertwined with our lives, shaping the choices we make and the world we're building for ourselves and future generations. That's what makes understanding it so important. AI is more than lines of code or fancy gadgets; it's a reflection of human creativity and ambition. And like anything we create, it brings questions and challenges along with its benefits.

This is where we start peeling back the layers. No tech-speak that'll make your head spin, no overcomplicated diagrams, just a clear, simple exploration of what AI is and how it fits into our world. This section is meant to spark your curiosity; to make you think about the ways AI is already part of your life and the ways it's changing the bigger picture of society.

Think about how you use technology every day, your smartphone, the apps you rely on, even the way you shop or communicate. AI is there, shaping these experiences behind the scenes. But it's also making an impact in ways that go far beyond convenience: how businesses operate, how we tackle global challenges like climate change, and even how we define fairness and ethics in a digital world.

So, let's dive in. This isn't just a crash course in what AI is; it's a chance to think about what it means for all of us. By the end of this part, you'll have a clearer understanding of not just the "what" of AI but also the "why" and the "how." And hopefully, you'll feel a little more equipped to engage with the world that AI is helping to shape.

Chapter 1: What is AI?

Imagine you have a magical helper who can think, learn, and assist you in many tasks. That magical helper is called Artificial Intelligence, or AI for short. But AI isn't magic, it's a very clever way of using computers to solve problems, make decisions, and even predict the future! Let's dive deeper to understand what AI really is, how it works, and how it's shaping the world around us.

What Is AI Really?

At its core, AI is about teaching computers to mimic how humans think and act. Think of it as giving machines the ability to:

1. **Learn from experience:** For example, a music app suggests songs you might like based on what you've listened to before.

2. **Solve problems:** Like a GPS app finding the fastest route to your destination.

3. **Understand language:** Chatbots that answer your questions online.

4. **See and recognize things:** Facial recognition in smartphones.

How Does AI Work?

AI is built using three key ingredients:

1. **Data:** AI needs lots of information to learn, like photos, text, or numbers.

2. **Algorithms:** These are like recipes that tell AI how to learn from the data.

3. **Computing Power:** Powerful computers help AI process information quickly.

Example: *Imagine teaching a computer to recognize a cat. Here's how it works:*

Data: *You show the AI thousands of pictures of cats.*

Algorithm: *The AI looks for patterns in the pictures, like whiskers, pointy ears, and fur.*

Learning: *Over time, the AI gets better at recognizing a cat, even in new pictures.*

Now let's Understand High Level: Types of AI

Not all AI is the same! Here are three levels:

1. **Narrow AI:** This is the most common type. It's good at one task, like recommending movies or playing chess.

2. **General AI:** This would be like a human, able to do many things well. Scientists are still working on this.

3. **Super AI:** This is a future concept where AI could be smarter than humans. It's still science fiction for now!

Key Technologies Powering AI

- **Machine Learning (ML)**: Teaching computers to learn from data without explicit programming.
  Example: Fraud detection in banking using supervised learning algorithms.

- **Deep Learning**: A subset of ML using neural networks to simulate human decision-making.
  Example: Autonomous vehicles leveraging convolutional neural networks (CNNs) to recognize objects on the road.

- **Natural Language Processing (NLP)**: Enabling machines to understand and generate human language.
  Example: ChatGPT crafting responses based on contextual understanding of text.

- **Reinforcement Learning (RL)**: Learning by trial and error to achieve goals.
  Example: AlphaGo mastering the game of

Go by iterating strategies to outperform human champions.

Practical Applications Beyond Basics

- **Healthcare**: AI-driven diagnostic tools, such as Google's DeepMind identifying eye diseases through retinal scans.

- **Retail**: Dynamic pricing systems predicting customer behavior and optimizing pricing in real-time.

- **Finance**: Algorithmic trading that makes decisions in microseconds based on market trends.

- **Transportation**: AI models predicting maintenance needs in fleet management.

Advanced Concepts in AI

- **Explainable AI (XAI)**: Systems that provide transparency in decision-making. **Example**: AI models explaining loan approval or rejection decisions.

- **Generative AI**: Creating new content such as images, text, or music. **Example**: DALL·E generating artwork from textual descriptions.

- **Transfer Learning**: Applying knowledge from one domain to another.
  Example: A model trained on language data being fine-tuned for medical transcription tasks.

Interactive Learning: Let's Try It Together

Activity 1: Think Like AI

Look around your room and name three objects.

Ask yourself: "What patterns make this object unique?" (e.g., a chair has legs and a seat.).

This is what AI does! It finds patterns to identify objects.

Activity 2: Be a Movie Recommender

Ask a friend to name their favorite movie.

Think about similar movies based on genre, actors, or storyline.

This is similar to how Netflix's AI recommends movies!

AI in Everyday Life

AI is everywhere, often in ways you don't even notice. Here are some examples:

- **Smart Assistants:** Siri or Alexa answering your questions.

- **Healthcare:** AI helping doctors detect diseases early.

- **Shopping:** Websites showing you products you're likely to buy.

- **Education:** Apps like Duolingo personalizing how you learn a new language.

The Bigger Picture: Why Does AI Matter?

AI isn't just about making life easier; it's about solving big problems:

- **Fighting Climate Change:** AI predicts weather patterns to plan renewable energy use.

- **Improving Accessibility:** AI tools help people with disabilities, like voice-to-text apps.

- **Boosting Creativity:** AI can compose music, write stories, or design artwork.

Looking Ahead: How Can You Shape AI?

AI is created and improved by people like you! Here's how you can get involved:

1. **Learn Coding:** Start with fun platforms like Scratch or Python.

2. **Explore AI Tools:** Try beginner-friendly AI tools like Teachable Machine by Google.

3. **Ask Questions:** Think about how AI can help solve problems in your community.

Did you know the first AI program was created in 1956? It was called "Logic Theorist" and could solve math problems.

AI can even beat humans at games like chess and go, which require complex strategies.

AI in Action: Combined Use Cases (Expanded for Better Understanding)

AI is transformative when multiple technologies and approaches are combined to solve complex problems. Here are three examples where AI operates in synergy to deliver real-world value:

1. Healthcare and NLP

Example: IBM Watson Health analyzing unstructured clinical notes for cancer treatment recommendations.

What's Happening Here?

- **Challenge**: Medical records, doctors' notes, and lab reports are often unstructured, meaning they're written in free-form text that computers can't easily process.

- **AI's Role**:

  - **Natural Language Processing (NLP)** is used to read and understand these unstructured documents, extracting key details such as patient history, diagnosis, and prescribed treatments.

- **Machine Learning** algorithms cross-reference this extracted data with vast medical research databases to identify the most relevant and evidence-based treatment recommendations.

- **Outcome**: Doctors receive a prioritized list of treatment options tailored to the patient's unique medical profile, significantly speeding up diagnosis and improving accuracy.

Impact: This approach helps oncologists keep up with the latest advancements in cancer treatment, reduces the risk of oversight, and ensures personalized care for patients.

2. Deep Learning in Security

Example: Identifying cyber threats using AI models that learn from network anomalies.

What's Happening Here?

- **Challenge**: Traditional security systems rely on predefined rules to detect threats, making them ineffective against new and sophisticated attacks.

- **AI's Role**:
  - **Deep Learning** models analyze vast amounts of network traffic data in real time.
  - By identifying patterns in normal network behavior, these models can spot anomalies—such as unusual login locations or sudden spikes in data usage—that might indicate a cyberattack.
  - Over time, these models learn and adapt to evolving threats, even predicting potential vulnerabilities before an attack occurs.

- **Outcome**: Faster detection and response to threats, minimizing potential damage from breaches.

Impact: This proactive approach to cybersecurity is critical for protecting sensitive data in industries like finance, healthcare, and government, where the cost of a breach can be catastrophic.

3. Retail with Reinforcement Learning

Example: Optimizing store layouts by analyzing customer navigation patterns.

What's Happening Here?

- **Challenge**: Retailers need to maximize sales by designing store layouts that encourage purchases, but customer behavior is dynamic and varies widely.

- **AI's Role**:

  - **Reinforcement Learning** is employed to test various store configurations in virtual simulations.

  - The system learns from these simulations, identifying which layouts encourage customers to spend more time in high-margin product areas.

  - **Computer Vision** and **IoT sensors** track real-world customer movements, refining the AI's model with actual behavioral data.

Outcome: Store managers get data-driven recommendations for shelving arrangements, product placement, and even aisle width to optimize customer flow and sales.

Impact: This method leads to higher customer satisfaction and increased revenue, as stores align their designs with shopper preferences and behaviors.

Why These Examples Matter

These combined use cases demonstrate how AI can solve intricate problems by integrating multiple technologies like NLP, deep learning, and reinforcement learning. This synergy:

- Enhances decision-making in critical areas like healthcare.

- Improves security in an increasingly digital world.

- Revolutionizes customer experiences in retail by aligning with real-world behavior.

Interactive Exercise: Imagine AI Solving a Problem in Your Life

Take a moment to think about a challenge you face in your daily life. It could be something small, like **finding your misplaced keys**, or something larger, like **reducing traffic congestion in your city**. Now, follow these steps:

1. **Write It Down**
   Clearly describe the problem you'd like AI to solve. Be as specific as possible. For example:

   - "I often lose my keys, and it takes me ages to find them."

   - "Traffic jams during rush hour make my commute stressful and inefficient."

2. **Imagine How AI Might Solve It**

   - For the misplaced keys: Picture a system where tiny Bluetooth trackers are attached to your keys. An AI-powered app maps your home, remembers the last location of the keys, and guides you to them using augmented reality.

   - For traffic congestion: Envision AI-powered traffic management systems analyzing real-time data from vehicles, traffic signals, and weather. The system dynamically adjusts signal timings and provides drivers with the most efficient routes to reduce congestion.

3. **Expand the Vision**
   Think of how the AI solution might work alongside humans to make the process smoother:

   - The key-finding app could suggest placing a bowl near the entrance for your keys, combining AI tracking with a behavioral nudge to build better habits.

   - The traffic system could integrate with public transport schedules, encouraging more people to use trains or buses when congestion peaks.

This exercise highlights an essential truth:

- AI isn't just about solving problems for us; it's about **enhancing our ability to solve them together**.

- For example, an AI traffic system doesn't just clear jams; it gives city planners insights to design smarter roads.

The **magic of AI** lies in this collaboration. It doesn't replace us; instead, it works alongside us to amplify human creativity, productivity, and problem-solving potential, enabling the extraordinary.

What challenge will you dream up for AI to solve today?

Conclusion

Artificial Intelligence is not an abstract, futuristic concept; it is a tool already shaping our world in meaningful ways. While it can appear complex, understanding its basics is essential to appreciate its potential. AI is about empowering machines to perform tasks that once required human intelligence, learning, reasoning, and decision-making. From simple recommendations on your streaming app to life-saving medical diagnoses, AI is woven into our daily lives.

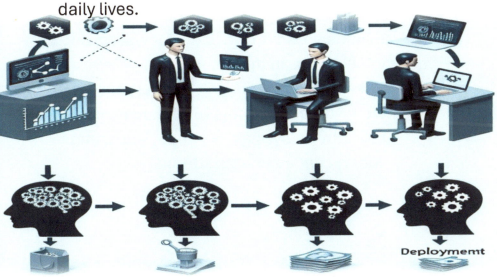

Chapter 2: AI and Society: Where Innovation Meets Humanity

Imagine this: the invention of the wheel didn't just improve transportation; it changed the very fabric of human civilization, enabling trade, exploration, and innovation. Today, **artificial intelligence (AI)** holds the same transformative potential. It's not just a tool; it's a revolution, subtly reshaping how we live, work, and solve the most complex challenges of our time.

How AI Integrates Into Everyday Life

AI is everywhere, often working behind the scenes to make life more convenient, efficient, and connected. Let's explore some examples that go beyond the obvious:

1. **Music Recommendations That Evolve With You:** Imagine you've been listening to upbeat tracks on Spotify for weeks, but lately, you're in the mood for something more relaxed. AI doesn't just suggest your old favorites; it adapts to your changing mood by analyzing the tempo, lyrics, and your recent listening patterns.

2. **Smart Grocery Shopping:** Grocery delivery platforms use AI to predict what you might run out of based on past purchases. It can even recommend recipes based on what's already in your fridge, reducing food waste and saving you time.

3. **AI-Powered Language Translation in Travel:** Planning to explore a country where you don't speak the language? Apps like Google Lens use AI to translate menus, signs, or even conversations in real time, breaking down language barriers and enriching cultural experiences.

4. **Climate Control in Smart Homes**: AI in smart thermostats learns your routine when you're home, asleep, or away. Over time, it optimizes energy use, cutting costs and reducing your carbon footprint without you lifting a finger.

5. **Sports Training and Analysis:** Athletes now have AI-driven tools to analyze their performance. Imagine an app that uses video analysis to recommend adjustments to your tennis swing or football kick in real time, helping you improve faster than ever.

AI's Impact on Work

AI is more than just automation; it's a partner in innovation.

1. **Streamlining Repetitive Tasks:** Imagine a software that processes thousands of invoices in minutes, flagging errors and ensuring accuracy. This frees up accountants to focus on strategic financial planning.

2. **New Professions and Industries:** AI has sparked entirely new fields like **robotics process automation (RPA)** or **virtual reality therapy**, creating opportunities for careers that didn't exist a decade ago. For instance, consider AI-powered fashion design, where algorithms predict upcoming trends and help designers create innovative collections.

3. **Collaborative Robots (Cobots):** In industries like manufacturing, cobots work alongside humans handling heavy lifting or precision tasks while people focus on creativity and oversight.

AI Solving Global Challenges

AI's power shines brightest when tackling society's most pressing problems:

1. **Sustainability**

   - **Smart Agriculture**: AI sensors in fields analyze soil health and predict crop yields, enabling farmers to optimize resources like water and fertilizer.

   - **Ocean Health**: AI-powered robots monitor marine ecosystems, identifying pollution hotspots and tracking endangered species.

2. **Healthcare**

   - **Mental Health Support**: AI chatbots provide immediate support for individuals dealing with stress or anxiety, offering coping techniques and connecting them to professionals if needed.

   - **Precision Medicine**: AI tailors treatments based on a patient's genetic makeup, increasing the success rates of therapies.

3. **Disaster Response**

- During natural disasters, AI analyzes satellite images to assess damage and prioritize areas needing urgent relief.

The Human Responsibility

With AI's power comes the responsibility to use it wisely.

- **Fairness**: How do we ensure that an AI hiring system treats all candidates equally?

- **Privacy**: Can we balance personalized services without overstepping boundaries on personal data?

- **Transparency**: Should AI systems explain their decisions, especially in life-altering scenarios like medical diagnoses or loan approvals?

This is where **you**, the next generation of innovators, come in. You have the opportunity to shape AI's future to ensure it empowers people, fosters equality, and drives progress.

Spot AI in Action: Look closely at your surroundings. Is your city using AI to optimize traffic lights or monitor air quality? Does your school or office use AI-based learning tools to personalize education or automate daily tasks? Maybe your favorite game uses AI to create smarter opponents. Discuss these examples with your friends, colleagues or classmates and explore how they impact your daily life.

Looking Ahead

AI isn't just about machines; it's about **people**. It's about designing systems that amplify human potential, solve problems, and open doors to new possibilities. As we move into the next chapters, you'll discover how you can actively participate in this exciting journey—armed with knowledge, curiosity, and a vision for a better, AI-driven world.

Task: Spotting AI in Your Daily Life

Objective: To help you identify and understand how AI is integrated into your everyday routines and its broader societal impact.

Instructions: Observe Your Day: Over the next 24 hours, pay attention to any interaction with technology. Note down where you think AI is involved. Examples could include apps, devices, or services you use.

Choose One Example: Pick the most interesting or impactful instance where AI played a role in your day.

Analyze the Impact: Reflect on how this AI-driven technology made your task easier, faster, or more enjoyable.

Part 2: AI for Global Challenges

When we think about the challenges facing our world today climate change, healthcare inequities, or the pressing need for better education—it's easy to feel overwhelmed. These aren't small problems, and they certainly don't have simple solutions. But here's a question worth considering: what if technology, specifically artificial intelligence, could help us tackle some of these massive global issues?

It's not just wishful thinking. AI is already proving that it can do more than make our lives convenient it can make a real difference where it matters most. Imagine algorithms predicting natural disasters in time to save lives, machine learning models optimizing the use of renewable energy, or AI-driven tools providing education to children in the most remote corners of the world. These aren't just possibilities they're happening right now.

This takes us into this space where technology meets humanity's most urgent needs. This isn't about fancy buzzwords or abstract concepts. It's about real stories, real innovations, and real impact. This part is where you'll see AI moving beyond the screen and stepping into the field whether it's helping researchers find better ways to fight climate change, assisting doctors in diagnosing diseases more accurately, or creating learning opportunities for kids who've been left behind by traditional systems.

What makes this all so exciting is how AI brings fresh thinking to these challenges. It's not here to replace human effort or compassion but to amplify them.

By analyzing vast amounts of data, recognizing patterns that humans might miss, and working tirelessly around the clock, AI offers tools that can supercharge the solutions we've been dreaming about for years.

But it's not just about the "wow" factor of what AI can do it's also about what it teaches us. These breakthroughs remind us that the biggest challenges can't be solved in isolation. They require collaboration across disciplines, countries, and communities.

AI is just one piece of the puzzle, but it's a powerful one that's helping.

So, as we explore this part of the journey, think of it as more than a showcase of AI's capabilities. It's also a call to action a reminder that the technology is here, and it's up to us to use it wisely, ethically, and in ways that genuinely make the world a better place. Whether it's protecting the planet, improving healthcare, or reimagining education, AI is showing us what's possible when innovation meets purpose. Let's dive in and see how AI is stepping up.

Chapter 3: Green AI: Harnessing Technology for a Sustainable Future

Climate change is one of the greatest challenges humanity faces, and artificial intelligence (AI) has stepped up as a transformative tool in this fight. Picture a world where machines predict extreme weather with unparalleled accuracy, optimize the use of renewable energy, and help restore ecosystems—all while working quietly behind the scenes. This isn't science fiction; it's our present reality.

How AI Powers Renewable Energy Solutions

AI is redefining how we generate and consume energy, maximizing efficiency and minimizing waste.

- **Solar and Wind Energy Optimization**: AI algorithms analyze weather forecasts, historical production data, and real-time conditions to predict energy output from solar panels and wind turbines. This ensures renewable energy sources operate at peak efficiency, even during fluctuating conditions.

Example: A solar farm in Spain uses AI to adjust the tilt of its solar panels in real time based on sunlight patterns, boosting energy production by 20%.

- **Smart Energy Grids**: AI powers intelligent grids that balance energy demand and supply. By predicting consumption trends and integrating renewables seamlessly, these grids reduce dependency on fossil fuels while cutting waste.

Example: In Denmark, AI integrates wind power into the national grid, ensuring the country meets over 40% of its energy needs from wind.

Reducing Carbon Footprints with AI

AI is advancing carbon capture and emissions reduction technologies, tackling climate change at its root.

- **Carbon Capture Innovations**: Researchers are using AI to design advanced materials that absorb CO_2 efficiently.

Example: CarbonCure Technologies employs AI to inject CO_2 into concrete during manufacturing. The CO_2 is permanently trapped, reducing emissions while making the concrete stronger.

- **Industrial Energy Savings**: AI optimizes energy use in large facilities.

Example: Google has leveraged AI in its data centers, reducing energy consumption for cooling systems by 40% through real-time adjustments based on data analysis.

AI's Role in Conservation and Biodiversity

AI is an indispensable tool for protecting our planet's ecosystems.

- **Deforestation Monitoring**: Drones equipped with AI can monitor forests in real time, identifying areas of illegal logging or land degradation.

Example: In the Amazon rainforest, AI-powered drones have reduced deforestation by providing rapid, actionable insights to local authorities.

- **Wildlife Protection**: AI analyzes patterns in poaching incidents and predicts where illegal activities are likely to occur. It also uses facial recognition for animals to track populations of endangered species.

Example: Conservationists in Africa use AI to monitor elephant movements, enabling rangers to intervene before poachers strike.

Optimizing Urban Sustainability

AI is helping cities become smarter and more sustainable:

- **Energy-Efficient Buildings**: Smart building systems powered by AI adjust heating, cooling, and lighting to save energy while maintaining comfort.

Example: In Singapore, AI-based systems have reduced energy consumption in skyscrapers by up to 30%.

- **Eco-Friendly Transportation**: AI enhances public transportation by analyzing traffic patterns, optimizing routes, and encouraging the use of electric vehicles.

Example: London's AI-driven traffic system has reduced congestion and pollution, improving air quality across the city.

Challenges and Ethical Considerations

While AI offers immense promise, it's not without challenges:

- **Energy Consumption of AI Itself**: Training AI models requires significant computational power, which can contribute to carbon emissions if not managed sustainably.

- **Equitable Access**: Developing nations may lack the resources to implement AI-driven solutions, potentially widening the gap in global climate efforts.

To address these challenges, researchers are exploring **"Green AI"**—developing energy-efficient algorithms and ensuring fair access to technologies worldwide.

Imagine AI in Climate Action

Think about your local community. What are some pressing environmental challenges it faces? Could AI help? For example:

- Could it manage waste more effectively?

- Could it reduce water consumption in agriculture?

Discuss these ideas with your peers or brainstorm ways to introduce AI-based solutions in your region.

Exercise: Innovating Local Solutions with AI

Step 1: Identify an Environmental Issue: Start by thinking about an environmental challenge in your community or region. Is it urban air pollution, water scarcity, excessive waste, or deforestation? Write down the problem and its most visible impacts.

Step 2: Imagine How AI Can Help: Brainstorm a solution that uses AI to address the issue. Consider these prompts to guide your thinking:

- **Data Collection:** Could AI collect and analyze data to better understand the problem?

- **Monitoring and Alerts:** Could AI-powered systems monitor the environment in real-time, sending alerts to prevent damage?

- **Prediction and Prevention:** Could AI predict future risks, such as floods or droughts, and help communities prepare?

- **Behavioral Change:** Could AI influence people's habits, such as reducing energy usage or recycling more effectively?

Step 3: Sketch Your Idea: Develop your idea into a simple concept. For example:

- A mobile app that uses AI to track air quality and suggests the least polluted times to exercise outdoors.

- An AI-powered drone network that monitors illegal dumping in rivers and alerts local authorities.

- A predictive model that helps farmers optimize water usage based on weather forecasts and soil conditions.

Step 4: Consider How It Works: Think about how your AI solution would function:

- What kind of data would it need?

- How would the AI process that data to provide actionable insights?

- Who would use the solution, and how would it benefit them?

Step 5: Reflect on the Impact: Once your idea is sketched out, answer the following questions:

- How would this solution improve the environmental issue?

- Could it be scaled to benefit other regions or communities?

- Are there any challenges, such as costs or accessibility, that need to be addressed?

Looking Ahead

AI is not a silver bullet, but it's a powerful tool that complements human ingenuity in addressing climate change. By harnessing its potential responsibly, we can create a greener, more sustainable future—one where technology doesn't just coexist with nature but actively works to protect it.

Chapter 4: AI and Healthcare: Saving Lives

Imagine a future where machines can diagnose diseases faster than any doctor, develop tailored treatments for individuals, or even predict pandemics before they happen. That future is now. AI in healthcare is not only transforming what's possible but is also saving lives and making medical care more accessible and equitable worldwide.

Revolutionizing Diagnosis

One of AI's most significant contributions is its ability to diagnose diseases with speed and accuracy. Unlike traditional methods, AI can analyze vast amounts of data in seconds, offering insights that were once unattainable.

- **Cancer Detection:** Advanced AI systems, like Google's DeepMind and PathAI, analyze medical images, such as X-rays and MRIs, to identify early signs of cancers like breast or lung cancer. Studies show that AI can detect anomalies sometimes missed by human doctors, providing patients with earlier interventions.

- **Cardiac Health:** AI tools can detect arrhythmias, heart valve issues, or even predict the likelihood of heart attacks by analyzing ECGs and wearable device data.

Pandemic Preparedness and Tracking: AI is playing a critical role in managing global health crises:

- **Outbreak Prediction:** During the COVID-19 pandemic, tools like BlueDot analyzed flight data, news reports, and health records to predict the virus's spread weeks before traditional models caught up.

- **Vaccine Development:** AI significantly accelerated the development of COVID-19 vaccines by identifying viable candidates and predicting their efficacy in record time.

Personalized Medicine

AI is unlocking the potential of treatments tailored specifically for individuals:

- By analyzing genetic information, lifestyle choices, and medical history, AI creates a "health fingerprint" unique to each patient.

- **Drug Development:** AI identifies potential molecules for drug treatments, drastically reducing the time and cost of development. For example, Insilico Medicine uses AI to discover new drugs, significantly shortening the research cycle.

- **Optimized Therapies:** In cancer treatment, AI helps identify which combinations of therapies, like immunotherapy and chemotherapy, are most effective for a specific patient.

Bridging Gaps in Underserved Areas

AI-powered solutions are transforming healthcare in remote and underserved regions:

- **Mobile Diagnosis:** Apps like Ada and Babylon Health empower community health workers to diagnose and suggest treatments for common conditions using AI chatbots and symptom checkers.

- **Diabetic Retinopathy Screening:** In India, tools like Google's AI model are being deployed to detect early signs of diabetic retinopathy in rural clinics, preventing blindness in thousands of patients.

Challenges and Responsibilities

While the potential of AI in healthcare is immense, it also raises crucial questions about privacy, data security, and bias. Who owns the data collected by these systems? How do we ensure AI recommendations are fair and unbiased? These are challenges that healthcare innovators must address as AI continues to reshape the field.

Case Study: Aidoc – Revolutionizing Emergency Medical Care with AI

In the fast-paced environment of emergency medicine, every second counts. Delayed diagnosis can mean the difference between life and death, especially in critical conditions like strokes, internal bleeding, or traumatic injuries. Aidoc, a pioneering healthcare AI company, is changing the game by using artificial intelligence to speed up and improve the accuracy of diagnostic imaging.

How Aidoc Works: Aidoc leverages advanced AI algorithms to analyze medical scans, such as CT and MRI images, in real-time. It detects anomalies like brain bleeds, pulmonary embolisms, or spinal fractures and flags them for immediate attention. By integrating seamlessly into existing hospital workflows, Aidoc enables radiologists and emergency physicians to act quickly and confidently, reducing the risk of human error during high-pressure situations.

1. **Impact on Stroke Diagnosis:** In stroke cases, rapid intervention is critical to minimizing brain damage and improving recovery chances. Aidoc's AI can:

   - **Detect Brain Bleeds:** By analyzing CT scans, it can identify intracranial hemorrhages in seconds, helping doctors decide whether to administer clot-busting drugs or proceed with surgery.

   - **Prioritize Scans:** Aidoc's system automatically flags critical cases, ensuring that radiologists address life-threatening conditions first, even in busy emergency departments.

   Real-World Example: A hospital in Texas reported that Aidoc reduced stroke diagnosis times by up to 60%, allowing patients to receive timely treatment and significantly improving their outcomes.

2. **Tackling Pulmonary Embolism (PE):** Pulmonary embolisms, which occur when blood clots block arteries in the lungs, are life-threatening but notoriously difficult to diagnose quickly. Aidoc's AI scans for signs of PE in chest CTs, providing instant alerts to radiologists.

Real-World Example 2: At a leading hospital in Israel, Aidoc detected a pulmonary embolism in a patient whose condition would have otherwise gone unnoticed until it was too late. The timely diagnosis saved the patient's life.

3. **Efficiency in Trauma Cases:** For trauma patients, especially those involved in accidents, internal injuries need immediate attention. Aidoc's AI detects:

- Fractures
- Organ damage
- Internal bleeding

Real-World Example: A trauma center in Germany integrated Aidoc's AI and reduced their critical diagnostic reporting time by 50%, enabling faster surgical interventions.

4. **Scaling AI in Emergency Departments:** Aidoc isn't just a tool for large hospitals; its scalability makes it valuable in smaller healthcare facilities. Rural hospitals, often lacking specialized radiologists, can rely on Aidoc's AI to bridge the gap by offering quick, expert-level analysis remotely.

Collaborative Success Stories: Partnership with Novant Health: Aidoc partnered with Novant Health in the U.S. to implement AI-powered tools across its network. Within months, radiologists reported reduced workload stress and faster decision-making for critical cases.

- **Deployment in the UK's NHS:** Aidoc's solutions were adopted in pilot programs by the National Health Service (NHS), where they helped reduce diagnostic backlogs and improve patient outcomes.

Broader Applications of Aidoc's AI: While the primary focus has been on emergency medicine, Aidoc is expanding its AI capabilities to other fields:

1. **Oncology:** AI identifies suspicious lesions in scans, aiding early cancer detection.

2. **Orthopedics:** Analyzing fractures and joint abnormalities, speeding up surgical planning.

3. **Cardiology:** Detecting heart abnormalities like aortic aneurysms or congenital defects.

Global Recognition: Aidoc has received numerous accolades for its impact on healthcare innovation, including being named one of TIME Magazine's "100 Best Inventions" in 2020. Its widespread adoption in hospitals worldwide demonstrates its success in merging cutting-edge technology with real-world medical needs.

The Path Ahead: Aidoc's story is just the beginning. As AI continues to evolve, its potential in emergency care will expand even further:

- **Predictive Diagnostics:** AI systems could anticipate complications before they occur, giving doctors a head start in prevention.

- **Remote Diagnostics:** Aidoc's tools could enable faster, more accurate diagnoses in telemedicine, reaching patients in remote areas.

- **Enhanced Training:** AI systems can serve as teaching tools for medical professionals, providing instant feedback on diagnosis and treatment plans.

Aidoc exemplifies how AI can transform healthcare by not just supporting but enhancing human expertise. It accelerates diagnosis, improves accuracy, and saves lives—proving that technology, when applied thoughtfully, can redefine what's possible in medicine. As hospitals around the globe adopt such innovations, the future of emergency care looks faster, smarter, and more precise than ever before.

Task: Become a Healthcare Innovator

Imagine you're tasked with solving a pressing health challenge in your community using AI. Follow these steps to turn your ideas into action:

1. **Identify a Health Challenge:**
   Think about common health issues in your area. Is it access to medical care in rural locations? Rising cases of lifestyle diseases like diabetes? Or perhaps delays in emergency response times?

2. **Brainstorm an AI Solution:**

- How could AI be used to address this problem?

- Could it be an app that monitors chronic conditions?

- Maybe a system that predicts local disease outbreaks?

- Or even an AI-powered chatbot that offers mental health support?

3. **Define How It Works:**
   Write a brief outline of your AI solution. Consider:

   - What data would it need?

   - How would it analyze that data?

   - How would people use it in their daily lives?

4. **Sketch Your Idea:**
   Create a quick diagram or storyboard showing how your solution would function. Include details like:

   - How users interact with it.

- The process behind the scenes (e.g., AI analyzing data, providing outputs).

- The desired outcome (e.g., better health outcomes, faster diagnosis).

5. **Think About the Impact:**
Reflect on how your solution could benefit your community. Ask yourself:

- Who would benefit the most?

- Could it improve access to care or reduce costs?

- What potential challenges might arise, like ethical concerns or privacy issues?

6. **Share Your Vision:**
Present your idea to friends, classmates, or family. Encourage them to ask questions, give feedback, or even build on your idea.

Example Prompts to Spark Ideas

For Rural Areas: *"What if we had an AI-powered telemedicine app that connects patients with doctors, even in areas with no nearby hospitals?"*

For Mental Health: *"Could AI analyze patterns in social media posts or wearable data to identify signs of stress or depression and offer early support?"*

For Emergency Response: *"How about an AI-driven system that analyzes real-time traffic and dispatches ambulances faster?"*

For Chronic Illness: *"Imagine a wearable device that uses AI to predict blood sugar levels and provides reminders to take action."*

Reflect and Discuss: Once you've developed your idea, reflect on its broader implications:

- Could your solution scale to other communities?

- How might it evolve as AI technology advances?

- Are there ethical considerations, such as ensuring fairness or protecting user data?

Looking Ahead

AI in healthcare is still in its early stages, but its impact is undeniable. From disease prevention to real-time emergency responses, AI is not just a tool—it's a partner in saving lives. As you explore this chapter, think about the countless ways AI can make healthcare smarter, faster, and more accessible for everyone. The future of medicine is here, and it's powered by AI.

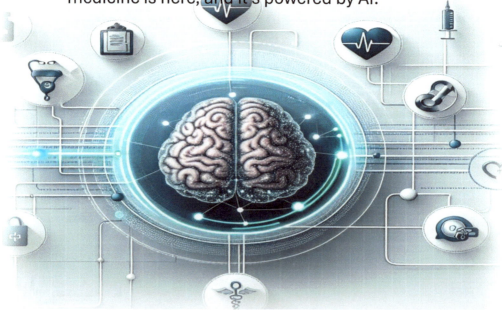

Chapter 5: AI - Redefining the Classroom, Inspiring the Future

Education is a powerful force for change, yet millions worldwide still lack access to quality learning. Artificial intelligence (AI) is rewriting this narrative, making education more accessible, personalized, and impactful than ever before. Imagine walking into a classroom where lessons adapt to your learning pace, strengths, and areas needing improvement. This tailored approach ensures that every student, regardless of background or ability, has the tools they need to succeed.

The Power of AI in Education: AI is addressing some of the most pressing challenges in education:

- **Personalized Learning:** AI-powered platforms like Smart Sparrow and Carnegie Learning use adaptive algorithms to analyze a student's progress and provide tailored learning experiences.

- **Global Accessibility:** AI translation tools such as Microsoft Translator enable students to access educational content in their native languages, bridging the language gap in multilingual classrooms.

- **Support for Educators:** From automating administrative tasks to providing detailed analytics on student performance, AI gives teachers more time to focus on teaching.

Case Study: Squirrel AI in China

Squirrel AI, an innovative education platform in China, uses AI to create hyper-personalized learning paths. By analyzing each student's knowledge base, learning pace, and problem-solving style, the system identifies strengths and weaknesses with pinpoint accuracy.

For example, if a student struggles with algebra but excels in geometry, Squirrel AI adjusts lessons to focus more on algebra, ensuring mastery without wasting time on concepts already understood. The platform is particularly impactful in rural areas, where teacher shortages are common, providing quality education to underserved communities.

Results:

- Students using Squirrel AI consistently outperform peers in traditional settings.

- Schools implementing Squirrel AI report improved teacher efficiency and higher overall engagement.

AI's Applications in Education

1. **Interactive Learning Tools:** AI powers immersive tools like Quizlet, which creates customized quizzes and flashcards for students. VR-based platforms like Alchemy VR allow students to explore subjects like history and biology in 3D, making learning engaging and memorable.

2. **Predictive Analytics:** AI systems predict at-risk students by analyzing attendance, grades, and engagement patterns. Schools use this data to intervene early, offering personalized support.

3. **Inclusive Education:** Tools like Otter.ai and Voiceitt assist students with disabilities by transcribing lectures in real time or converting text into speech for better accessibility.

Exercise: Rethinking Education with AI

Let's spark your creativity with a fun and reflective activity:

1. **Identify an Education Challenge:** Think about a specific problem in education within your community. Examples include:

   o Limited access to teachers.

   o Students falling behind in certain subjects.

   o Lack of resources for special education.

2. **Imagine an AI-Powered Solution:** How could AI tackle this problem? Could it be an app that:

   o Translates lessons into local languages.

   o Offers real-time tutoring in math or science.

   o Helps teachers identify struggling students faster.

3. **Design a Concept:**

- **Name your AI tool:** What would you call it?

- **Features:** What key features would it include?

- **Impact:** How would it improve education in your community?

4. **Present and Discuss:** Share your idea with a group. Gather feedback, refine your concept, and imagine how it could be scaled to other communities.

Real-World Inspiration: The Khanmigo AI Assistant

Khan Academy introduced **Khanmigo**, an AI-powered teaching assistant that acts as a tutor and coach for students. For teachers, Khanmigo provides insights into classroom trends and individual student progress, enabling targeted interventions.

How it works:

- Students type in questions, and Khanmigo guides them to the answer instead of providing it outright.

- *Teachers receive real-time analytics, including which concepts need reinforcement and which students may require additional support.*

Results: Khanmigo has made learning more interactive and efficient, empowering both students and educators.

Educators Empowered by AI

AI doesn't just transform learning for students, it revolutionizes teaching for educators:

- **Automated Grading:** Platforms like Gradescope grade assignments and exams using AI, saving countless hours.

- **Lesson Planning Assistance:** AI suggests activities and resources tailored to the curriculum.

- **Enhanced Engagement:** Tools like Classcraft gamify the classroom experience, using AI to reward student progress and encourage participation.

Future of AI in Education

The possibilities for AI in education are vast:

- **Cultural Exchange:** AI-powered virtual classrooms connect students from different countries, fostering global collaboration.

- **Lifelong Learning:** AI recommends courses and career paths for adults seeking to upskill.

- **Green Education:** AI tools like "Green School AI" track energy usage in schools and suggest sustainable practices for students to learn environmental responsibility.

A Project Idea: Innovate Your Education Idea

Think big about how AI could transform education in your community!

Step 1: Identify a gap. For instance, are students in rural areas missing out on science labs?
Step 2: Visualize a solution. What if an AI-based VR app simulated

lab experiments for remote students?
Step 3: Create a pitch. Write down how your idea works, its benefits, and who would use it.
Step 4: Share your innovation. Host a mini "pitch event" with friends or classmates to present your ideas.

Exercise: If you could design an AI tool for your school, what would it do? Would it help with homework, provide virtual reality lessons, or connect students from different countries? Sketch your idea and share it with your peers.

By transforming education, AI ensures that knowledge is not a privilege but a right, empowering every learner to reach their full potential.

Interactive Exercise: Imagine Your AI-Powered Educational Tool

Step into the shoes of an innovator! What kind of AI tool could revolutionize learning in your school or community? Let your imagination guide you as you design a solution that addresses real educational needs.

Step 1: Identify a Problem: Think about challenges in your school or community:

- Do students struggle with understanding difficult concepts?

- Are there language barriers that make learning harder?

- Is access to teachers or resources limited in any way?

Step 2: Envision an AI-Powered Solution: Create a tool that addresses the problem. Here are some ideas to spark your creativity:

- **Homework Helper:** A chatbot that explains tricky questions step by step without giving away the answer.

- **VR Classrooms:** An AI-powered virtual reality app where students can explore historical sites, dive into the ocean, or travel through space.

- **Global Connection Platform:** A tool that matches students with peers from different countries to collaborate on projects, practicing language skills and cultural exchange.

- **Special Needs Assistant:** An app that uses speech-to-text, predictive text, or visual aids to help students with learning disabilities excel in class.

- **Career Mentor AI:** A system that analyzes students' skills, interests, and aspirations to recommend future career paths and relevant subjects.

Step 3: Bring Your Idea to Life: Sketch out your idea or write a short description. Include:

- **The tool's name:** A creative and memorable name that captures its purpose.

- **Key features:** What does it do? What problems does it solve?

- **Target users:** Who would benefit most— students, teachers, or both?

- **Impact:** How will it transform learning and make education more engaging?

Step 4: Share and Discuss: Present your idea to your peers or family:

- Gather feedback on what they love and what could be improved.

- Brainstorm additional features that could make the tool even better.

- Reflect on how the tool could be adapted for different schools or communities.

Step 5: Dream Bigger: Think beyond your school. How could this AI tool help learners globally? Would it work in rural schools, urban areas, or even for lifelong learners?

Example Ideas and Tools to Inspire You

- **EcoLearn AI:** An app that teaches environmental science through gamified lessons. Students earn points by solving real-world problems like designing eco-friendly cities or managing virtual forests.

- **BridgeLang AI:** A translation tool that allows multilingual classrooms to learn together, ensuring inclusivity for all language speakers.

- **Project Pal:** A virtual group project assistant that assigns roles, tracks progress and mediates conflicts to ensure smooth teamwork.

Redefining Education

AI IS NOT A REPLACEMENT FOR HUMAN TEACHERS BUT A PARTNER THAT EMPOWERS THEM TO DO MORE. It personalizes learning for students, enhances teaching efficiency, and breaks barriers that once seemed insurmountable. As we look to the future, AI in education offers endless opportunities to transform lives and unlock the full potential of every learner.

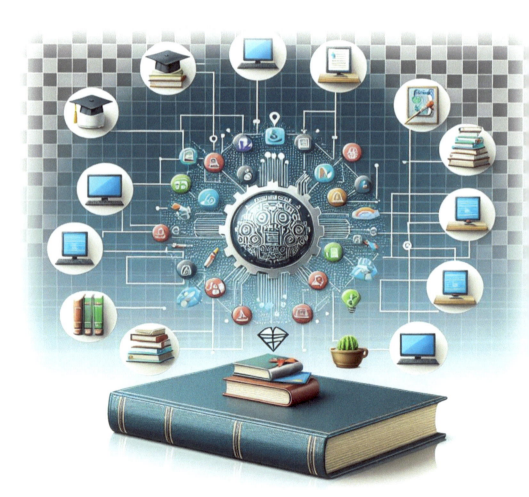

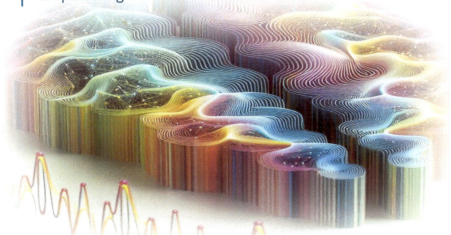

Part 3: Building the Future

We've seen what AI is and how it's already helping to tackle some of the world's most pressing challenges. But here's the question that matters most: what's next? For AI, for society, and most importantly for you.

The truth is, AI isn't just something created by a select group of experts in far-off labs. It's a tool, a field, and a way of thinking that anyone can engage with. Whether you're an aspiring technologist, an artist curious about how AI can spark creativity, or someone passionate about ethics and fairness in technology, there's space for you in this world. The future of AI isn't just being built by engineers—it's being shaped by people from every discipline, background, and perspective.

This part is all about empowerment. This section is your invitation to dive into the world of AI, not just as an observer but as an active participant. Whether you're taking your very first steps or wondering how your unique skills and interests can play a role in the AI ecosystem, this is where the journey begins.

We'll start with the basics of getting hands-on with AI no intimidating jargon, no prerequisites, just practical ways to start learning and experimenting. From there, we'll explore the ethical questions that sit at the heart of AI development. After all, creating technology without considering its impact can lead to tools that harm rather than help. Understanding and championing ethical AI isn't just important it's essential if we want AI to be a force for good in the world.

And here's something you might not expect you don't need to be a coder to have a meaningful career in AI. This part of the journey shines a light on the incredible variety of roles available in this space. From product design to journalism, from

AI ethics to user experience, there's a place for everyone to contribute to this fast-evolving field.

Think of this as a blueprint for possibility. You don't need to have all the answers right now. All you need is curiosity and a willingness to explore. The world of AI is growing fast, and the skills, ideas, and voices you bring to the table can help shape its future. Whether you're building the next big AI tool, driving conversations about fairness and ethics, or finding creative ways to use AI in unexpected places, you're part of a movement that's just getting started.

So, let's look ahead. The future of AI isn't something to fear—it's something to build. Together.

Chapter 6: Embarking on the AI Journey: Where Possibilities Begin

AI is no longer just a concept of the future. It's here and it's transforming the world as we know it. But how do you go from understanding AI in theory to actually building your own AI applications? This chapter will guide you through the process step by step, ensuring that you not only understand AI but also get the hands-on experience to start creating your own projects. You don't need a Ph.D. or a high-end computer— just curiosity, dedication, and the right resources.

Understanding the Basics: What You'll Need

Before diving into the tools and platforms, let's briefly go over the essential building blocks you'll need to start your AI journey:

1. **Basic Knowledge of Programming:** If you are completely new to programming, it's important to familiarize yourself with basic concepts such as loops, variables, functions, and data structures. Python is the most commonly used language in AI

development due to its simplicity and versatility. You can start learning Python from platforms like:

- **Codecademy** (for beginners)
- **Python.org** (official documentation)
- **Real Python** (tutorials and exercises)

2. **Understanding the Concept of Machine Learning:** Machine learning (ML) is the backbone of AI. It involves training algorithms to learn patterns from data. You don't need to be an expert to begin, but understanding the basic concepts such as supervised learning, unsupervised learning, and neural networks will be incredibly helpful. Free online resources like **Coursera** (Andrew Ng's ML course) or **Google's Machine Learning Crash Course** are fantastic places to start.

Step 1: Choose Your First AI Project: Before you start building, it's important to have a clear goal in mind. Don't worry about making something complex right away. Keep your first project simple and fun. Here are some ideas to get you started:

- **AI to recognize plants from pictures:** You can build a model that can identify different types of plants when you take a photo.

- **AI chatbot:** Create a basic AI chatbot that can hold simple conversations with users, responding to specific questions or prompts.

- **Weather prediction AI:** Using historical weather data, build a simple AI model to predict tomorrow's weather based on patterns from the past.

Step 2: Choose the Right Tool: You don't need expensive hardware to start developing AI models. Below are some beginner-friendly tools that will get you started, along with specific instructions on how to use each.

1. *Teachable Machine by Google:*
   Teachable Machine is one of the easiest ways to begin working with AI. It doesn't require any coding knowledge and is completely accessible through your browser.

How to Use Teachable Machine:

1. *Go to Teachable Machine.*

2. *Select **Get Started** and choose a type of model you want to build (Image, Audio, or Pose).*

3. *For image classification, for example, you can upload images of objects or plants and train the model to recognize them. You can teach the AI to differentiate between various categories (e.g., cats vs. dogs).*

4. *Once you've uploaded your images, click **Train Model**. Teachable Machine will use the images to build a model that can identify new photos you upload.*

5. *You can download the model to use it in your own applications or even share it with others.*

Interactive Task:
Use Teachable Machine to create a plant identifier. Collect images of 3-4 different types of plants and train the AI to recognize them. Once done, test the model by uploading new photos of the plants.

2. TensorFlow

TensorFlow is one of the most powerful AI frameworks out there. While it's more complex than Teachable Machine, it provides a more comprehensive learning experience and deeper control over your models.

How to Get Started with TensorFlow:

1. **Install TensorFlow:**
   First, you need to install TensorFlow on your machine. Follow the official installation guide here. You can run TensorFlow in Google Colab (a cloud-based notebook environment) or set it up on your local machine.

2. **Start with a Simple Tutorial:**

   - *Go to TensorFlow's tutorial page.*

   - *Choose a beginner-friendly tutorial like "Basic Classification: Classify images of clothing." This tutorial will walk you through building a model to recognize different types of clothing (e.g., shirts, pants, etc.).*

3. *Understand the Basics of a TensorFlow Model:*

- ○ **Data Pipeline:** *You'll first learn how to load and prepare data for training your model. TensorFlow uses datasets like MNIST (handwritten digits) to help beginners get started.*

- ○ **Model Building:** *In this tutorial, you'll use a neural network model to learn patterns in your data.*

- ○ **Training:** *After building your model, you will train it by feeding it data. The AI will adjust its internal parameters to learn how to make predictions.*

Interactive Task: *Follow the tutorial to build your own image classifier using TensorFlow. After finishing the tutorial, create a model to recognize everyday objects like coffee mugs, shoes, and books.*

3. *Scratch for AI*

If you're new to coding or are looking for a fun, interactive way to learn AI concepts, Scratch for AI is perfect for you. This visual programming language lets you build simple AI projects without needing to write code.

How to Use Scratch for AI:

1. *Go to Scratch and sign up for an account.*

2. *Use **Scratch for AI** to create projects. You'll be using blocks to build logic instead of writing code.*

3. *Follow interactive tutorials to create AI models, such as chatbots or simple games that learn based on your actions.*

4. *You can combine this with **machine learning for kids** by using the Scratch extension "ML for Kids" to introduce machine learning concepts in a simple, engaging way.*

***Interactive Task:** Create a project where Scratch learns to play a game based on your actions. For example, create a game where the AI learns how to move a character on the screen to avoid obstacles.*

Step 3: Learn by Doing - Step-by-Step Process: Building your first AI model is about experimenting, learning from your mistakes, and iterating on your work. Here's a simple process to follow when building any AI model:

1. **Gather Data:** Data is the foundation of AI. Depending on your project, gather a dataset. You can find free datasets on websites like:

   - Kaggle

   - UCI Machine Learning Repository

   - Google Dataset Search

2. **Preprocess the Data:** Data often needs to be cleaned and formatted before it can be used. You'll need to:

   - Remove any irrelevant or duplicate data.

   - Normalize the data (scaling it to a standard range).

   - Split the data into training and test datasets.

3. **Choose Your Model:** Select an AI model based on your problem. For instance:

- **For image classification:** You can use a convolutional neural network (CNN).

- **For predicting numerical values:** Use a linear regression model.

4. **Train Your Model:** Training involves feeding data into the model so it can learn from it. You'll likely use platforms like TensorFlow or PyTorch to train your models. The model will adjust its parameters to minimize errors in predictions.

5. **Evaluate the Model:** After training, assess how well your model performs using a test dataset. Evaluate its accuracy, precision, and recall (depending on your project). If the results aren't satisfactory, tweak your model or gather more data.

6. **Deploy the Model:** Once you're happy with your model, deploy it for real-world use. You can integrate it into an app, a website, or even a chatbot.

Step 4: Explore and Expand Your Learning: AI is a vast field, and the more you explore, the more exciting it becomes. Here are ways to keep learning:

- **Join AI Communities:** Connect with AI enthusiasts (e.g Nitin Panwar) and experts on platforms like **Kaggle**, **Reddit's r/Machine Learning**, or **AI Discord servers**.

- **Participate in Competitions:** Once you're comfortable with AI, participate in challenges like **Kaggle competitions** to solve real-world problems and learn from others.

- **Work on Larger Projects:** As your skills grow, try building more complex models, like self-driving car simulators, recommendation systems for movies or music, or AI-based predictive analytics tools.

Remember: AI is a journey that requires patience, experimentation, and a willingness to learn from your mistakes. With time, you'll build your confidence, tackle more complex projects, and develop the skills needed to create powerful AI applications. So, dive in, start building, and enjoy the process! The world of AI is waiting for you to explore and create.

Chapter 7: Ethics in AI Development – Building Technology with Responsibility

AI holds immense potential to revolutionize industries and improve lives. However, this power comes with the responsibility to ensure that AI is developed and used ethically. Ethical considerations in AI are not just theoretical concerns; they directly affect how systems perform, how users trust them, and how society benefits from them. This chapter dives deep into key ethical challenges, practical solutions, and actionable steps for creating responsible AI systems.

Why Ethics in AI Matters: Ethics in AI is critical because AI systems often impact people's lives in areas such as hiring, healthcare, financial decisions, and law enforcement. An AI system that is biased, opaque, or invasive can have far-reaching consequences, amplifying inequalities and eroding trust.

Let's break down the key areas where ethics play a role in AI:

Key Ethical Considerations in AI Development

1. Bias: Addressing the Hidden Prejudices

AI systems learn from data, and if the data is biased, the AI will inherit those biases. For example:

- **Hiring Discrimination:** In 2018, an AI hiring tool was found to favor male applicants because it was trained on data from a male-dominated workforce. This reinforced existing gender biases rather than leveling the playing field.

- **Facial Recognition:** Studies have shown that some facial recognition systems perform poorly for darker-skinned individuals because they were trained on predominantly lighter-skinned datasets.

How to Mitigate Bias:

- Collect diverse and representative datasets.

- Use fairness testing tools like **IBM AI Fairness 360** and **Fairlearn**.

- Regularly audit models for bias, especially in sensitive applications.

2. Transparency: Opening the AI "Black Box"

AI decisions can sometimes seem like a mystery to end users, especially with complex algorithms like deep learning. However, lack of transparency can undermine trust and accountability.

Example: A loan application system rejects an applicant but provides no explanation. This can lead to frustration and accusations of unfairness.

How to Ensure Transparency:

- Implement **Explainable AI (XAI)** techniques, which provide insights into how decisions are made.

- Develop systems that allow users to question and understand AI outputs.

- Ensure decision-making processes are documented and accessible for audits.

3. Privacy: Protecting Personal Data

AI systems often require vast amounts of data, much of which may be sensitive. Mishandling this data can lead to breaches, misuse, and loss of user trust.

Example: Social media apps often collect user data to improve recommendations. However, improper data handling can lead to leaks, as seen in the infamous **Cambridge Analytica** case.

How to Protect Privacy:

- Use privacy-preserving techniques like data anonymization and differential privacy.

- Limit data collection to what is strictly necessary.

- Adhere to global privacy regulations, such as **GDPR** and **CCPA**.

Practical Steps to Build Ethical AI Systems

Step 1: Ask the Right Questions

At every stage of development, ask:

- Who might be affected by this AI system?

- Are there underrepresented groups in the training data?

- Could this system unintentionally cause harm or reinforce stereotypes?

Step 2: Test for Bias and Fairness

- Use tools like **AI Fairness 360**, **Fairlearn**, or **Google's What-If Tool** to detect biases in your models.

- Test your models with diverse real-world scenarios to uncover potential blind spots.

Step 3: Collaborate with Diverse Teams

Inclusion leads to better outcomes. By involving individuals from varied backgrounds, you're more likely to identify ethical concerns early on.

- Incorporate ethicists, sociologists, and domain experts into your team.

- Hold regular cross-disciplinary reviews to evaluate the ethical implications of your projects.

Step 4: Adopt Ethical Frameworks

Leverage established AI ethics guidelines, such as:

- **EU's Ethics Guidelines for Trustworthy AI**

- **IEEE's Ethically Aligned Design**

- **Google's AI Principles**

Case Study: Lessons from an AI Hiring Tool

In 2018, a major tech company developed an AI tool to automate hiring decisions. However, the system disproportionately penalized resumes that included the word "women" (e.g., "women's soccer team") because it was trained on historical data from male-dominated industries.

Key Takeaways:

1. *Training data must be scrutinized for historical biases.*

2. *Regular audits can catch unintended consequences early.*

3. *Diverse teams bring fresh perspectives to prevent oversights.*

Reflection: Spotting Bias in AI Applications

Think about an AI application you interact with daily, such as:

- Virtual assistants (e.g., Alexa, Siri)

- Recommendation systems (e.g., Netflix, Spotify)

- Social media feeds

Reflect on these questions:

- Does the application work equally well for everyone, regardless of background?

- Can you identify examples where its recommendations might be biased?

- What steps could the developers take to improve fairness and inclusivity?

Example Reflection

Consider a music recommendation system. If a user frequently listens to music from underrepresented genres, the system might struggle to make accurate recommendations due to insufficient data. To address this, developers could include a wider variety of genres in the training dataset.

The Path Forward: Ethics as a Core Principle

Ethical AI development isn't just about ticking boxes; it's about embedding fairness, transparency, and accountability into every stage of the process. By following these principles:

- AI systems can better serve diverse populations.

- Developers can build trust with users.

- Companies can avoid reputational risks and legal challenges.

By prioritizing ethics, you're not only creating better technology but you're contributing to a more just and equitable society. Let's lead the way in building AI that benefits everyone, without leaving anyone behind.

Chapter 8: Careers in AI for Every Discipline – Shaping the Future Across Fields

Artificial Intelligence (AI) is not confined to coding and engineering; it's a multidisciplinary domain that offers opportunities to individuals from all walks of life. Whether you're passionate about art, healthcare, justice, or education, there's a place for you in the world of AI. This chapter explores career paths in AI, how to prepare for them, and what the future holds for AI professionals.

AI Career Paths: Diverse Roles for Every Passion

AI's applications are vast, and so are its career opportunities like AI scientist, AI developer, AI transformation etc. Here's an in-depth look at some exciting future roles, what they entail, and who they're best suited for:

1. AI Ethics Specialist

- **What They Do:** AI ethics specialists focus on ensuring that AI systems are fair, unbiased, and align with societal values.

They tackle challenges like algorithmic bias, data privacy, and transparency.

- **Who It's For:** Ideal for individuals passionate about justice, human rights, and ethical decision-making.

- **How to Get Started:**
  - Study topics like data ethics, philosophy, and policy-making.
  - Familiarize yourself with frameworks like GDPR, IEEE Ethics Standards, and the EU AI Act.
  - Pursue certifications like AI Ethics by CertNexus or courses on Coursera.

2. AI Product Designer

- **What They Do:** Combine technical expertise with user-centered design to create intuitive and accessible AI applications, such as voice assistants or personalized learning platforms.

- **Who It's For:** Perfect for those with a creative flair and an interest in technology and user experience (UX).

- **How to Get Started:**
  - Learn design tools like Figma, Sketch, or Adobe XD.
  - Study UX/UI design principles and basic AI concepts.
  - Build a portfolio of projects, such as mockups for AI-powered apps.

3. AI Journalist

- **What They Do:** Translate complex AI topics into engaging stories that inform and educate the public. They explore AI's societal impact, breakthroughs, and ethical concerns.

- **Who It's For:** Great for writers and communicators with a curiosity for technology.

- **How to Get Started:**
  - Hone your writing skills with a focus on tech journalism.
  - Start a blog or contribute to platforms like Medium.
  - Study AI fundamentals to explain topics like machine learning, neural

networks, and automation effectively.

4. Data Storyteller

- **What They Do:** Use data visualization and storytelling to transform complex AI insights into actionable narratives that businesses can use.

- **Who It's For:** A role for those who love working with numbers but also have a knack for storytelling and creativity.

- **How to Get Started:**

    o Learn data visualization tools like Tableau, Power BI, or Python libraries like Matplotlib.

    o Study storytelling techniques to make your data insights compelling.

    o Take courses on data analysis and AI basics.

Case Study: Merging Technology and Storytelling

Meredith Broussard, a journalist and AI researcher, exemplifies the intersection of technology and storytelling. Her work focuses on the societal impacts of AI, emphasizing how technology can reinforce inequalities if not developed responsibly. Her insights highlight the importance of multidisciplinary approaches in AI.

How to Start Your AI Journey: Step-by-Step Guide

1. Identify Your Passion: AI intersects with nearly every discipline. Ask yourself:

- Are you interested in **creative fields** like art, writing, or design?

- Do you enjoy working with **data and numbers**?

- Are you passionate about **social issues**, such as equality and justice?

- Does the idea of advancing **healthcare, education, or sustainability** excite you?

2. Explore Multidisciplinary Fields: AI applications span industries:

- **Healthcare:** Develop AI models to detect diseases or manage hospital workflows.

- **Education:** Design adaptive learning platforms that cater to individual student needs.

- **Law:** Use AI for contract analysis, legal research, or ensuring compliance with regulations.

- **Environmental Science:** Build AI systems that monitor and reduce carbon footprints.

3. Build Your Skills: Start with foundational skills tailored to your chosen path:

- **Technical Basics:** Learn Python, data analysis, or machine learning frameworks like TensorFlow.

- **Domain Knowledge:** Dive deep into the industry you're passionate about (e.g., healthcare, law, or education).

- **Soft Skills:** Develop critical thinking, problem-solving, and communication skills.

4. Gain Hands-On Experience: Practical projects can set you apart:

- Participate in **AI hackathons** or coding competitions.

- Contribute to **open-source AI projects** on GitHub.

- Build your portfolio with projects like chatbots, recommendation systems, or AI-powered tools relevant to your field.

5. Network and Collaborate: Join platforms like **Kaggle**, **AI-focused LinkedIn groups**, and **meetup events**.

- Attend **AI conferences**, webinars, and workshops to connect with mentors and peers.

- Collaborate on interdisciplinary projects to gain diverse perspectives.

The Future of AI Careers: Where the Field is Heading

1. Democratization of AI: As tools become more accessible, individuals with non-technical backgrounds will play a larger role in designing and managing AI systems.

2. Human-Centered AI Roles: Roles focusing on the societal impact of AI, such as AI Ethics Officers or AI Behavioral Analysts, will grow as ethical considerations take center stage.

3. Integration Across Industries: AI's influence will expand into new sectors, from agriculture to entertainment, creating niche career opportunities.

4. Lifelong Learning: With AI evolving rapidly, professionals will need to engage in continuous learning through certifications, workshops, and online courses.

Interactive Activity: Map Your AI Career Path

1. **Self-Reflection:**

   - What are your strengths?

   - Which industries or problems excite you most?

   - What role aligns with your personality and goals?

2. **Action Plan:**

   - Pick one AI-related skill to learn this month.

   - Identify three resources (books, courses, or mentors) to support your journey.

- Set a goal to complete one hands-on project within the next three months.

3. **Collaborate:** Share your goals with peers and brainstorm ideas for AI projects in your field of interest.

Closing Thoughts

AI is not just a career path; it's a transformative force shaping the future of every industry. Whether you're a writer, designer, scientist, or advocate, or anyone, there's an opportunity for you to contribute. By combining your passion with AI's capabilities, you can create solutions that impact the world. Start small, stay curious, and let your unique perspective guide you toward an AI career that's as dynamic as the field itself.

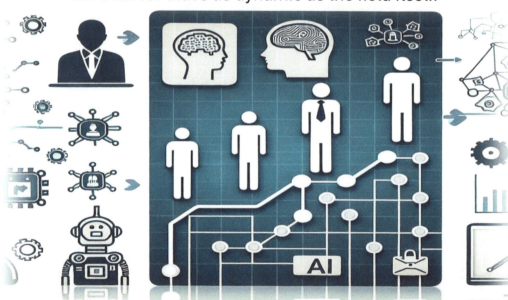

Part 4: Interactive and Hands-On

So far, we've explored what AI is, how it's shaping the world, and how you can start building your own future within this field. But let's be honest—nothing makes a subject come alive quite like rolling up your sleeves and getting your hands dirty. That's what this part is all about: turning concepts into action.

This part is where you stop just reading about AI and start *creating with it*. Don't worry—this isn't about diving into a sea of complex math or impenetrable code. Instead, it's about discovering just how approachable AI can be. Think small, manageable projects that help you grasp big ideas. Imagine building a simple chatbot that answers questions, or an AI tool that analyzes emotions in text. These aren't just fun experiments; they're stepping stones that connect the theory of AI to its practical applications.

But we're not stopping there. AI isn't a field that stands still, and neither should we. This part also invites you to think ahead—to look at the trends and technologies that are already reshaping how we'll live, work, and collaborate in the years to come. From the intriguing possibilities of quantum AI to the evolving role of AI in global decision-making, the future is bursting with opportunities to imagine and innovate.

Here's the exciting part: these aren't just abstract ideas for experts to work on. They're openings for you to dream big, experiment, and contribute your unique perspective.

By engaging with these hands-on projects and forward-thinking discussions, you'll see firsthand how small actions today can ripple outward into larger possibilities tomorrow.

Empowering the Next Generation

This isn't about mastering AI overnight—it's about starting where you are and building from there. Whether you're coding a simple project, brainstorming futuristic applications, or just exploring how AI connects to your own passions, this section is designed to make the journey accessible and rewarding.

So, grab your curiosity and a willingness to tinker, because it's time to make AI personal.

Let's create, innovate, and imagine what's next together.

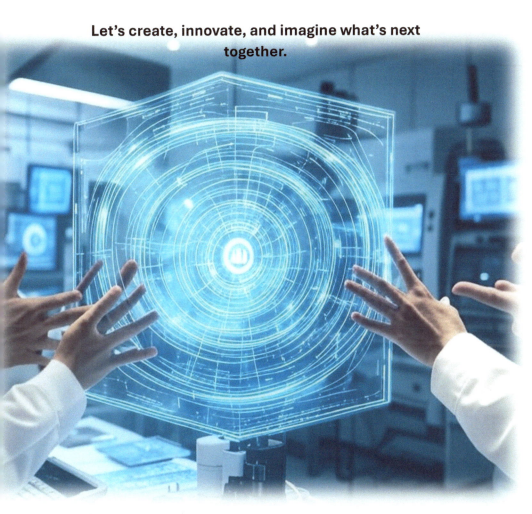

Chapter 9: Mini AI Projects for Students – Hands-On Learning in AI

Now that you've explored AI's potential, it's time to roll up your sleeves and dive into practical applications. This chapter introduces step-by-step guides to creating simple yet impactful AI projects. These projects are designed to give you hands-on experience while sparking your creativity to explore more advanced possibilities.

Detailed Mini Projects in AI

Project 1: Build Your Own Chatbot

- **Goal:** Create a chatbot that can engage users with basic conversation.

- **Tools Needed:** Python, libraries like NLTK or spaCy, and a free chatbot framework like Rasa or ChatterBot.

- **Steps:**

  1. **Install Required Tools:** Install Python and relevant libraries (pip install nltk rasa).

2. **Preprocess Text Data:** Use NLTK to tokenize and clean user inputs.

3. **Define Responses:** Create a set of question-answer pairs or an intent-response mapping.

4. **Train the Chatbot:** Use a chatbot framework like Rasa to build conversational logic.

5. **Test and Improve:** Interact with your chatbot and expand its knowledge base with additional intents and responses.

- **Interactive Add-On:**

  o Give the chatbot a unique personality, like a virtual chef, travel guide, or gaming assistant.

  o Integrate speech-to-text libraries like Google's Speech API for voice interactions.

Project 2: Sentiment Analysis Tool

- **Goal:** Determine the sentiment of text data, such as tweets or customer reviews.

- **Tools Needed:** Python, scikit-learn, pandas, and datasets like IMDB reviews or Twitter data.

- **Steps:**

  1. **Collect and Label Data:** Download labeled datasets (e.g., positive and negative reviews).

  2. **Preprocess Data:** Clean the text (remove stop words, punctuation, and apply stemming).

  3. **Train a Model:** Use scikit-learn's TfidfVectorizer to convert text into numerical data and train a model (e.g., Logistic Regression).

  4. **Evaluate Performance:** Test your model on new text samples and calculate accuracy.

  5. **Visualize Results:** Use libraries like Matplotlib or Seaborn to display sentiment trends over time.

Project 3: Sustainability Calculator

- **Goal:** Create a tool to estimate the environmental impact of common activities.

- **Tools Needed:** Python or Excel, open-source sustainability datasets.

- **Steps:**

  1. **Define Metrics:** Choose metrics like energy consumption, carbon footprint, or water usage.

  2. **Design Formulas:** Create mathematical models for different activities (e.g., driving a car, eating meat).

  3. **Build a User Interface:** Use Excel forms or a Python-based web framework like Flask for user input.

  4. **Generate Reports:** Provide a summary of the user's impact, with suggestions for improvement.

  5. **Expand Data Sources:** Integrate live APIs, such as CO_2 emission calculators.

- **Interactive Challenge:** Present your tool to peers, gather feedback, and iterate based on suggestions.

Additional Mini Projects for Advanced Exploration

Project 4: Personalized Study Companion

- **Goal:** Develop an AI tool that creates personalized study plans and quizzes based on a student's performance.

- **Tools Needed:** Python, TensorFlow/Keras, and user interaction data.

- **Steps:**

  1. **Data Collection:** Start by gathering a dataset of practice questions, topics, and performance metrics.

  2. **Recommendation Engine:** Build an AI model to analyze user performance and recommend areas for improvement.

  3. **Dynamic Quiz Generation:** Use GPT-based APIs (like OpenAI's) to create custom quizzes tailored to the user's weak areas.

  4. **Feedback Loop:** Provide detailed performance reports and progress tracking.

- **Advanced Add-On:** Integrate speech recognition to offer spoken quizzes and feedback.

Project 5: AI-Powered Virtual Art Gallery

- **Goal:** Create an AI tool that curates and generates artwork based on user preferences.

- **Tools Needed:** Python, TensorFlow, and generative models like GANs (Generative Adversarial Networks).

- **Steps:**

    1. **Dataset Creation:** Collect images of artwork from various styles (e.g., Impressionism, Abstract).

    2. **Preference Input:** Create a simple interface for users to select their favorite styles.

    3. **Art Curation:** Use a recommendation algorithm to display similar artworks from your dataset.

    4. **Artwork Generation:** Train a GAN to generate original art pieces inspired by user preferences.

     5. **Interactive Gallery:** Build a virtual gallery using HTML/CSS or 3D visualization libraries like Three.js.

- **Advanced Add-On:**
  - Enable users to print their generated artwork on merchandise like posters or mugs.
  - Incorporate augmented reality (AR) to visualize art in physical spaces.

Project 6: AI Resume Analyzer

- **Goal:** Build a tool to analyze resumes and provide tailored feedback.
- **Tools Needed:** Python, NLP libraries like SpaCy, and resume datasets.
- **Steps:**
  1. **Text Extraction:** Parse resumes using libraries like PyPDF2.
  2. **Keyword Matching:** Match skills and experiences to job descriptions.
  3. **Feedback Generation:** Generate tailored recommendations for improvement (e.g., adding certifications, restructuring layout).

4. **Visualization:** Provide a scorecard with charts to display strengths and areas for improvement.

- **Interactive Add-On:** Integrate job-matching APIs like LinkedIn or Indeed to recommend relevant job postings.

Project 7: AI-Driven Language Learning App

- **Goal:** Create an app to help users learn a new language with vocabulary games and quizzes.

- **Tools Needed:** Python, Flashcard libraries (like Anki), and APIs for translation (like Google Translate).

- **Steps:**

  1. **Vocabulary Database:** Build a database of words, phrases, and translations.

  2. **Quiz Mechanism:** Create multiple-choice or fill-in-the-blank quizzes.

  3. **Speech Recognition:** Use tools like SpeechRecognition to evaluate pronunciation.

4. **Progress Tracking:** Include gamification elements like badges and leaderboards.

- **Advanced Add-On:** Use AI to analyze a user's pronunciation and offer corrective feedback in real time.

Project 8: Virtual Fitness Coach

- **Goal:** Design an AI tool to recommend personalized fitness routines and track progress.

- **Tools Needed:** Python, fitness datasets, and computer vision frameworks like OpenCV.

- **Steps:**

  1. **User Profile Creation:** Collect data on age, weight, fitness goals, and preferences.

  2. **Routine Recommendation:** Use a decision tree or recommendation algorithm to suggest workouts.

  3. **Pose Detection:** Integrate OpenCV to analyze workout form using a webcam.

4. **Feedback System:** Provide real-time guidance and track calorie burn.

- **Interactive Add-On:**

  - Include virtual challenges where users can compete with friends.

  - Integrate wearables like Fitbits for additional metrics.

Closing Thoughts: The Power of Hands-On Learning

These mini projects provide a starting point to experiment with AI. Each one is an opportunity to apply theoretical knowledge, build practical skills, and discover your interests.

Empower your curiosity and let AI be the canvas for your imagination, every task you tackle shapes the future you'll create. Explore, experiment, and evolve!

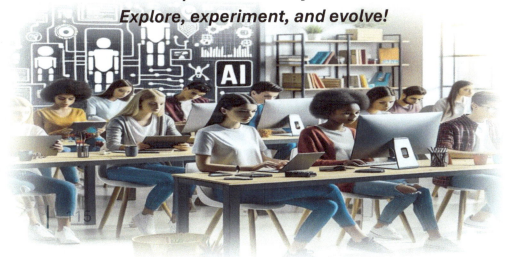

Chapter 10: The Road Ahead: Exploring the Next Frontiers of AI

Artificial Intelligence isn't a static field—it's a constantly evolving frontier of human ingenuity and technological prowess. The next era of AI promises to be transformative, not just in terms of innovation but also in how it integrates into our lives and reshapes industries, societies, and even our understanding of intelligence itself. In this chapter, we'll delve into some of the most exciting and impactful trends shaping the future of AI.

1. AI-Human Collaboration: Redefining Partnership

The future of AI isn't about replacement; it's about augmentation. Imagine a world where humans and AI work together as partners, each complementing the other's strengths.

Practical Applications:

- **Healthcare Revolution:** AI tools like IBM's Watson Health analyze vast medical datasets to assist doctors in diagnosing diseases more accurately and rapidly, enabling personalized treatment plans.

- **Creative Arts:** Platforms like DALL·E and MidJourney allow artists to create stunning visual narratives by simply describing their vision in text. The result? A fusion of human imagination and machine precision.

- **Scientific Discovery:** AI systems such as AlphaFold are decoding the mysteries of protein structures, accelerating breakthroughs in drug development and biotechnology.

Case Study:

In 2022, an artist used AI to co-create a digital artwork that sold for $432,500 at Christie's auction house. The AI wasn't just a tool—it became a collaborator, generating elements of the piece while the artist curated and refined the final output.

Reflection Point:
Think about your daily life or work. How could an AI assistant enhance your creativity or productivity? What tasks could it take on to free up your time for deeper thinking?

2. Quantum AI: The Next Computational Leap

While classical computers rely on bits, quantum computers use qubits, enabling them to process exponentially more information. When paired with AI, quantum computing could solve problems previously thought insurmountable.

Emerging Applications:

- **Supply Chain Optimization:** Imagine a logistics network with millions of interconnected variables—quantum AI can find the most efficient routes and schedules in seconds.

- **Pharmaceutical Innovation:** AI-driven simulations powered by quantum computing could reduce drug development timelines from years to months, saving countless lives.

- **Climate Modeling:** Predicting climate change impacts with unprecedented accuracy, aiding in proactive global responses.

Example in Action

Google's Sycamore processor achieved "quantum supremacy" in 2019 by solving a problem in 200 seconds that would take the world's fastest supercomputer 10,000 years. While this was a test case, it highlights the potential of quantum AI in tackling real-world challenges.

Interactive Question: *If quantum AI became widely available tomorrow, what industry or challenge would you apply it to? How might it change the way we think about problem-solving?*

3. AI for Global Governance: Enhancing Decision-Making at Scale

AI's ability to analyze vast datasets and predict patterns could make it a cornerstone of future governance systems. By augmenting human decision-making, AI can address global challenges with unprecedented precision and speed.

Key Possibilities:

- **Disaster Mitigation:** AI systems like One Concern use predictive analytics to model and reduce the impacts of earthquakes, floods, and wildfires.

- **Conflict Resolution:** By analyzing geopolitical trends and proposing neutral solutions, AI could facilitate global diplomacy and peace-building efforts.

- **Transparent Governance:** AI-powered platforms can audit government spending, highlight inefficiencies, and detect corruption, ensuring accountability.

Case Study:

The United Nations has begun exploring AI applications for achieving its Sustainable Development Goals (SDGs). For instance, AI tools are being deployed to monitor deforestation and illegal fishing, helping to preserve biodiversity.

Interactive Exercise: What global issue matters most to you—climate change, poverty, education? Jot down ways AI could address this issue. How might you contribute to such initiatives in the future?

4. Personalized AI: Tailoring Technology to You

As AI advances, it's becoming increasingly personalized, learning from individual preferences and behaviors to deliver tailored experiences.

Examples of Personalization:

- **Education:** AI-powered platforms like Khan Academy and Duolingo adapt lessons to a learner's pace and style, enhancing educational outcomes.

- **Healthcare:** Wearable devices like Fitbit or Apple Watch use AI to provide real-time health insights, enabling proactive care.

- **Retail:** E-commerce giants like Amazon and Alibaba employ AI to predict customer needs, offering personalized shopping recommendations that feel almost intuitive.

Thought Experiment: Imagine having your own AI "life coach" that learns your habits, goals, and challenges. How might it transform your productivity, health, and relationships?

5. Ethical AI: Building Trust in Technology

As AI becomes more powerful, ensuring it remains ethical and unbiased is critical. The future of AI depends on transparency, accountability, and inclusivity.

Key Ethical Challenges:

- **Bias Mitigation:** Ensuring AI doesn't perpetuate or amplify societal biases. For example, efforts are underway to make facial recognition systems more accurate across diverse populations.

- **Privacy Protection:** Striking a balance between data utility and individual privacy. Tools like differential privacy enable companies to analyze data without exposing personal details.

- **Autonomous Decision-Making:** Defining clear boundaries for AI in critical areas like law enforcement and military applications.

Initiative Spotlight: The Partnership on AI, involving tech giants like Google, Microsoft, and OpenAI, focuses on creating ethical guidelines for AI development and deployment.

Interactive Challenge: How would you ensure ethical AI development in your field of expertise? What values or principles would you prioritize?

What This Means for You

The future of AI isn't just about the technology itself—it's about how we choose to use it. As future innovators, leaders, and citizens, we have the power to shape AI's role in creating a better, more equitable world.

Key Takeaways:

- Stay curious: Continuously learn about AI's evolving capabilities and implications.

- Be proactive: Advocate for ethical and responsible AI practices in your community or workplace.

- Think big: Dream about how AI can solve problems that matter to you and the world.

Closing Reflection:

The future of AI is in your hands. What legacy will you leave in this era of transformation? How will you harness the power of AI to build a better tomorrow?

Bonus Projects: AI for Everyone: No Coding Required

Here are some creative and beginner-friendly AI project ideas that don't require coding skills but still showcase the transformative power of AI:

1. AI-Enhanced Personal Scrapbook

Objective: Create a beautiful digital scrapbook of memories using AI tools for photo enhancement and design.

Steps to Follow:

1. **Collect Photos:**

   - Gather digital photos from your phone, camera, or computer. These can be family moments, travel shots, or special events.

2. **Enhance Photos with AI:**

   - Use tools like **Fotor** or **Adobe Express**. These platforms let you enhance photo quality, adjust brightness, and even apply artistic filters effortlessly.

3. **Design the Layout**:

   - Use a drag-and-drop tool like **Canva** or **Crello**.

   - Explore AI-suggested templates based on your theme (e.g., birthdays, vacations).

4. **Add AI-Generated Captions**:

   - Use **ChatGPT** to craft creative captions for your photos.

   - Example Prompt: "Write a fun caption for a family dinner photo."

5. **Compile into a Scrapbook**:

   - Organize your enhanced photos and captions in a logical sequence (e.g., chronologically or thematically).

   - Export the final design as a PDF or share it digitally with friends and family.

Learning Outcome: Discover how AI simplifies photo editing and design to turn memories into stunning visuals.

2. Interactive AI-Powered Learning Guide

Objective: Build an interactive guide on a topic using user-friendly AI tools.

Steps to Follow:

1. **Choose a Topic:**

   o Select a subject you're passionate about (e.g., space, dinosaurs, or cooking).

2. **Research the Topic:**

   o Use AI-powered research tools like **Elicit** to gather interesting facts and data quickly.

3. **Create Interactive Content:**

   o Use platforms like **ThingLink** or **Canva for Education:**

      ▪ Upload images or infographics related to your topic.

      ▪ Add clickable hotspots with text, audio, or video explanations.

4. **Include Dynamic Quizzes:**

- o Use AI tools like **Kahoot!** or **Quizizz** to design engaging quizzes and embed them in your guide.

5. **Publish and Share**:

- o Export the project as a web link or PDF for easy sharing with friends and classmates.

Learning Outcome: Learn how AI enhances educational content creation to make learning fun and accessible.

3. AI-Personalized Recipe Book

Objective: Curate a recipe book tailored to specific dietary preferences.

Steps to Follow:

1. **Set a Theme**:

- o Decide on the type of recipes you want to include (e.g., vegan, gluten-free, or quick meals).

2. **Generate Recipes**:

- o Use **Whisk AI** or **Spoonacular**:

- Input ingredients or preferences, and let the AI suggest creative recipes.

3. **Organize Recipes**:

   o Categorize recipes into sections (e.g., breakfast, lunch, dinner).

   o Include prep times, difficulty levels, and nutritional information.

4. **Design the Recipe Book**:

   o Use tools like **Canva** with AI-suggested layouts.

   o Add AI-generated meal photos using platforms like **DeepAI's Food Image Generator**.

5. **Export and Share**:

   o Save as a digital PDF or print a physical copy for your kitchen.

Learning Outcome: See how AI simplifies meal planning and recipe personalization.

4. AI for Music Moodboards

Objective: Curate a moodboard combining visuals, music genres, and emotions.

Steps to Follow:

1. **Select a Theme:**

   o Choose a theme for your moodboard (e.g., "Relaxing Evening" or "Upbeat Morning").

2. **Research Music Genres:**

   o Use AI-powered tools like **Musicovery** or **Every Noise at Once** to explore genres that fit your theme.

3. **Create Visuals:**

   o Use AI tools like **Canva** to design a moodboard with:

     - Genre names.

     - Icons, colors, and photos that represent the mood.

4. **Add Music Suggestions:**

   o Use platforms like **SongLink** to generate links to songs or playlists matching your theme.

5. **Finalize and Share:**

   o Export your moodboard as an image or PDF and share it on social media.

Learning Outcome: Explore how AI connects music, visuals, and emotions for creative projects.

5. AI Art and Story Fusion

Objective: Create a series of AI-generated artworks that narrate a visual story.

Steps to Follow:

1. **Define Your Story Theme**:
    - Decide on a theme or plot (e.g., "The Journey of Seasons" or "A Robot's Adventure").

2. **Generate Artwork**:
    - Use AI art tools like **DeepArt** or **Artbreeder** to create visuals for each part of the story.
    - Experiment with different styles to match the mood of the narrative.

3. **Write Captions**:
    - Use AI writing tools like **ChatGPT** to create engaging captions for each artwork.

- Example Prompt: "Write a 50-word description of an artwork showing a futuristic cityscape."

4. **Compile the Story**:

- Organize the artworks and captions into a slideshow or PDF using **Canva**.

5. **Share the Experience**:

- Present your visual story to friends or on platforms like Behance.

Learning Outcome: Combine AI's artistic and storytelling capabilities for impactful narratives.

6. AI-Powered Eco-Tracker

Objective: Build a personalized tracker to monitor and improve eco-friendly habits.

Steps to Follow:

1. **Set Up a Tracker**:

- Use **Notion AI** to create a custom template for tracking habits like recycling, energy usage, and water conservation.

2. **Input Data**:

- o Log daily or weekly data (e.g., "number of plastic bottles recycled").

3. **Analyze Patterns**:

   - o Use Notion AI's analysis features to identify trends and receive suggestions.

4. **Set Goals**:

   - o Use AI to generate realistic and actionable eco-friendly goals (e.g., "Reduce water usage by 10% in one month").

5. **Visualize Progress**:

   - o Create charts and visual summaries to track improvement.

Learning Outcome: Understand how AI supports sustainability and habit-building.

7. AI World Explorer

Objective: Create an interactive travel guide featuring lesser-known global destinations.

Steps to Follow:

1. **Pick Destinations**:

- Use **Google Earth Studio** or **Atlas Obscura** to identify unique travel spots.

2. **Gather Information**:

   - Use AI tools like **ChatGPT** or **Bing AI** to collect cultural trivia, history, and travel tips.

3. **Design the Guide**:

   - Use **Canva** or **Prezi** to create an interactive presentation with:

     - Images, fun facts, and maps.

     - Local cuisine and activity suggestions.

4. **Include Interactive Features**:

   - Embed videos, clickable links, and itineraries.

5. **Publish and Share**:

   - Share your guide as a digital PDF or web link.

Learning Outcome: Experience AI's power in curating and presenting diverse global information.

Your AI Journey Awaits!

Artificial intelligence isn't just for coders, it's for creators, dreamers, and innovators like you!

The best part? You don't need to know programming to explore its endless possibilities. With simple, user-friendly tools, you can design stunning visuals, create interactive guides, or even build personalized eco-trackers.

Each project you try unlocks a new way of thinking and inspires fresh ideas. Start small, stay curious, and let AI be your partner in creativity. Dive in, experiment, and remember, every step you take expands what you believe is possible!

Let's dial up the humor

Here are some lighter, more playful takes on AI not knowing what it is:

AI is like a confused toddler who can solve complex math problems but still can't figure out how to tie its own shoes.

AI doesn't know what AI is... It just keeps doing stuff and hopes someone figures it out.

AI is like that friend who's always busy, but when you ask what they're doing, they just say, 'I'm processing...

AI is like your pet hamster in a maze—occasionally it makes great decisions, but sometimes it just runs into walls.

AI doesn't know what AI is—it's like asking a calculator, 'What are you?' and it responds with, 'I'm... numbers.

If you ask AI what it is, it might just respond with, 'I'm still working on that, but hey, I can beat you at chess!

AI is like that guy at the party who knows a lot but can't explain where he got his knowledge from. He's just... really good at Googling.

AI is the ultimate self-doubter—it knows a lot but constantly asks, 'Is this what I'm supposed to be doing?

AI doesn't know what AI is... but it's pretty sure it's better at Scrabble than you.

AI is like a detective who's always solving mysteries but never knows what the crime is.

AI might not have feelings, but it definitely knows how to make you feel like you're always one step behind.

AI's greatest strength? Understanding you, even when you don't understand yourself.

AI is the friend who always has advice but never knows what to do with their own free time.

AI is like a personal assistant who remembers everything, except where you left your keys.

Why did the AI apply for a job? It wanted to improve its net worth.

AI can help you plan a trip to Mars, but it still can't figure out why your printer won't connect.

AI is like the most enthusiastic librarian—always ready to give you the perfect answer, even if you didn't ask for it.

AI could be the next Shakespeare, but for now, it's still struggling with understanding why your 'to-do' list is never complete.

AI: Always ready with the answer, unless the question is 'What's the meaning of life?' Then it recommends a reboot.

Becoming AI Changemakers

As we conclude this journey through the transformative world of artificial intelligence, one thing is abundantly clear: AI is not just a tool; it's an ally in creating lasting, meaningful change. Whether you're a student, a professional, or simply curious about what AI can do, remember this AI is a reflection of how we choose to shape the future.

Your Role in Shaping the Future: The insights and skills you've gained are just the beginning. This book was crafted not only to introduce you to the fascinating possibilities of AI but also to inspire you to see AI as a partner in solving the world's biggest challenges.

Imagine the impact you could have:

- **Combat Climate Change:** Design AI-driven systems that reduce waste and improve energy efficiency.

- **Healthcare for All:** Use AI to bring diagnostics and personalized treatments to underserved communities.

- **Revolutionize Education:** Create learning platforms powered by AI, ensuring every child, no matter where they live, has access to quality education.

The possibilities are endless, and the first step begins with you.

Why Your Voice Matters: The future of AI is not only about technological breakthroughs; it's about *people*. Your decisions today, whether as a designer, developer, policymaker, or educator will shape the systems and solutions of tomorrow.

- **Prioritize Fairness:** Ensure that AI systems treat everyone equitably.

- **Champion Transparency:** Advocate for AI solutions that are open and understandable.

- **Promote Inclusivity:** Develop tools and platforms that bridge gaps rather than widen them.

Your creativity, curiosity, and compassion will be the driving forces behind AI's role as a force for good.

Moving Forward: A Call to Action

What's next for you? The possibilities are endless, but here are some ways to take your first steps:

1. **Start Small:** Pick a project that excites you—build a chatbot, create a playlist, or explore AI ethics.

2. **Stay Curious:** Follow advancements in AI, read widely, and seek out mentors who inspire you.

3. **Collaborate:** Connect with others who share your passion for AI, including myself, the author of *Humintel*.

Every journey begins with a single step, but with each action, you'll grow closer to becoming an AI changemaker.

Connect With Me: Let's Shape the Future Together

I firmly believe that AI is for everyone. Whether you're an absolute beginner or someone eager to deepen your understanding, you're part of this transformative movement. Read *Humintel*, to understand how AI can complement human potential and creativity.

If you have questions, ideas, or simply want to share your journey, I encourage you to reach out. Together, we can explore how to use AI as an ally, not just in technology, but in building a better, fairer, and more sustainable world.

Final Words

This book is not the end of your journey, it's the starting point of an incredible adventure. You hold the power to shape not just the future of AI but the future of our world.

Be bold. Stay passionate. Dream big. Whether it's one idea, one project, or one innovation at a time, you have the power to make a difference.

Go out there, embrace AI as your ally, and create the world you envision.

The future isn't about AI surpassing us; it's about AI empowering us to reach heights we never imagined. Together, we are the architects of a limitless tomorrow

– Nitin Panwar

www.ingramcontent.com/pod-product-compliance
Lightning Source LLC
LaVergne TN
LVHW072049060326
832903LV00053B/300